Windy Days

By Jennifer S. Burke

Welcome
Books

Children's Press
A Division of Grolier Publishing
New York / London / Hong Kong / Sydney
Danbury, Connecticut

Photo Credits: Cover, pp. 7, 9, 11, 15, 17, 19, 21 by Angelo Barros and Nelson Sa: p. 5 © Index Stock Photography, Inc.: p. 13 © Neil Rabinowitz/Corbis
Contributing Editor: Mark Beyer
Book Design: Nelson Sa

Visit Children's Press on the Internet at:
http://publishing.grolier.com

Library of Congress Cataloging-in-Publication Data

Burke, Jennifer S.
   Windy days / by Jennifer S. Burke.
    p. cm. — (Weather report)
   Includes bibliographical references and index.
   Summary: Describes what a windy day is like and some of the things that the wind can do.
   ISBN 0-516-23122-7 (lib. bdg.) — ISBN 0-516-23047-6 (pbk.)
   1. Winds—Juvenile literature. [1. Winds.] I. Title.

QC931.4.B86 2000
551.51'8—dc21

                              00-024584

Contents

It's very **windy** today.

Wind can **blow** things around.

This flag is waving in the air.

Windy days are good days to blow soap bubbles.

I hold my bubble stick in the air.

The wind blows through the holes and makes bubbles.

7

Last week we went to the park for a **picnic**.

Our blanket would not stay flat.

The wind picked up the blanket's edge.

The wind blew away our paper plates.

Windy days aren't great days for a picnic.

Sailboats need wind to move them across the water.

The wind fills their **sails**.

Sailboats move fast on windy days.

Windy days make trees **sway**.

Tree **branches** rub together.

I can hear the wind moving through the trees.

15

We have **wind chimes** in our backyard.

The wind knocks the chimes together.

The chimes ring when the wind blows.

17

When it is windy you have to hold onto things.

People can lose their hats on windy days.

19

Windy days are best for **kite** flying.

My kite flies high in the air.

New Words

blow (**bloh**) to move quickly by air

branches (**branch**-ez) the parts of a tree that stick out and have leaves

kite (**kyt**) a wood and plastic toy that flies in the wind

picnic (**pik**-nik) a lunch at the park

sailboats (**sayl**-bohts) a boat that moves with help from the wind

sails (**saylz**) parts of a sailboat that catch the wind to move the boat

sway (**sway**) to blow back and forth

wind (**wihnd**) air that moves

wind chimes (**wihnd chymz**) hanging metal pieces that ring as the wind bangs them together

windy (**wihn**-dee) when air is moving

To Find Out More

Books
Can You See the Wind?
By Allan Fowler
Children's Press

Feel the Wind
By Arthur Dorros
HarperCollins Children's Books

Web Sites
Dan's Wild Wild Weather Page
http://www.whnt19.com/kidwx/
Here you can learn all you need to know about the weather.

Winds and Weather
http://tqjunior.advanced.org/5818/globalwinds.html
Learn what causes wind and other facts about wind.

23

Index

About the Author
Jennifer S. Burke is a teacher and a writer living in New York City. She holds a master's degree in reading education from Queens College, New York.

Reading Consultants
Kris Flynn, Coordinator, Small School District Literacy, The San Diego County Office of Education

Shelly Forys, Certified Reading Recovery Specialist, W.J. Zahnow Elementary School, Waterloo, IL

Peggy McNamara, Professor, Bank Street College of Education, Reading and Literacy Program